Horseplay Secrets

Learning

in

Rhyme

from

Equines Sublime

By

Linda Ann Nickerson

Horseplay Secrets

Learning in Rhyme from Equines Sublime

Gait
House
Press

Published in the United States by Gait House Press.

Printed in the United States of America.

2014

ISBN: 0615975062

ISBN-13: 978-0615975061

Illustrations

Cover Illustration:
Young Horses,
copyrighted by Linda Ann Nickerson.

Horse Icon
Public domain artwork.

Dedication

This collection of verses is dedicated fondly to the ever-increasing and incurably happy herd of horse-loving friends with which I have been blessed.

Each of you has enriched my life and my appreciation for all things horse in innumerable ways.

You know who you are.

Ride on, posse.

Author's Preface

Horse lovers carry heart secrets that run deeper than others may ever understand.

Our memories are filled with special equines with whom we have shared moments that marked our souls forever.

We carry vestiges of triumphs and tears, happiness and hurt. In an instant, we can recount both solemn and silly situations. Mostly, we bear an enduring tenderness we can hardly explain – all because we live with these marvelous creatures.

If you love horses, you are probably already nodding your head.

Some onlookers may perceive our

equestrian pursuits as daring endeavors, skilled competitions or some form of art. To others, our horseplay may look like simple sport, mere recreation, or just another kind of exercise. A few may even question our sanity, as we seem to pour all we have, both time and treasure, into our horses.

Occasionally, horse lovers may appear to engage in ridiculous rowdiness, as we cavort with these beloved animals in their own element.

And that may be so.

But we know there's much more to it.

Horseplay is character-building and life-affirming. Hacking around with horses and engaging in equine interaction, whether for fun or for sport, teaches us countless lessons for this life and the next.

Any long-time equestrian can readily recount experiences when certain horses lifted spirits, eased life's stresses, or broke hearts.

Surely, our equine counterparts can carry us to glory ... or bring us down a few pegs.

Horseplay Secrets: Learning in Rhyme from Equines Sublime is aimed at sharing some of these stories and truths.

For horseplay is never just play – if we're paying attention. Sweet secrets are there to be shared between horse and human.

Come along for the ride. Join me in the laughter, the tears, the learning, the occasional silliness, and the ever-present wonder of horseplay.

Linda Ann Nickerson

Contents

1   Come to Me   5

2   A Gentle Touch (Basking   6
Beats Tasking)

3   My Daughter's First Love (A   7
Poetic Lead Line on Her Best
Valentine)

4   Far Afield (A Limericked   9
Ride 'Cross the Countryside)

5   Land Mines   11

6   Detangling with Delight   12
(Rhyming Lots on Losing
Knots)

7   Midwinter Mirth (A   14
Limericked Word on My
Favorite Herd)

8   El Santo (Saddled with   15
Responsibility)

9 Paging the Prime   17
   Veterinarian (Three
   Questions in Rhyme on a
   Horse Past Her Prime)

10 Dandy Day   20

11 Gearing Up (A Limericked   21
    Ride on a Colt with Pride)

12 Launched Again (An   23
    Acrostic in Rhyme)

13 Bally-hue   25

14 Have You Herd? (A Rhyme   27
    Past-Due on a Wonderful
    Crew)

15 Royalty Spoilty (Limericked   29
    Joy for a True Blue Boy)

16 Fragile Finery (The Cost of   31
    Grace and Glory)

17 A Cloud Unveiled   33

18 Great Green Grub   36

19 No Wrest for the Wicked   37

20 Belly Up to the Bale (A   38
    Rhyming Form Amid the
    Storm)

21 Private Dining (A Filly's   40
    Rhyme on Suppertime)

22 Fairly Fall (A Trip on the   41
    Trail)

23 A Great Sport (Poetic Scan   42
    from a Loyal Fan)

24 Halter-Skelter (Wisdom   44
    from the Wild)

25 My Guy (A Simple List to   46
    Give the Gist)

26 Jumpin' Jehosaphat   48
    (Limericked Sweeps on a
    Horse That Leaps)

27 Private Moments (Recalling   49
    the Birth of a Foal)

28 Reunion Aloft (Farewell to a   52
    Friend)

29 Jump Start on Smarts   54

30 A Stroll That's Droll   55

31 Stocking Up (A Rhyming   56
    Ridge Too Close to the
    Bridge)

32 Minis and Whinnies   58
    (Limericked Courses on
    Tiny Horses)

33 Just Arrived (A Foal Extols   60
    an Outdoor Stroll)

34 A Daily Dip   61

35 First Flight   63

36 Green Lessons (A Poetic   65
    Reflection on Riding
    Correction)

37 Running with the Right   67
    Herd

38 Still Standing   70

39 Sight-Mare (Seeing Through   72
    Blindness)

40 Untacked in Fact   75

41 From the Dust   77

42 A Running Start (Lyrics   78
    Penned for a Truest Friend)

43 Low Maintenance (A Poetic   81
    Presuming on Personal
    Grooming)

44 Playing It Cool   85

45 Ready to Go   86

46 The Master's Marvel   88

47 My Lifeguard   89

48 Mystified   91

49 Rescued by the Ride   92

50 My Dirty Secret   93

51 Bee-ware (A Limericked   95
    Scheme on a Near-Broken
    Dream)

52 Stardust and Snowflakes (A   98
    Winter's Day for Bay and
    Gray)

53 Capping It Off   100

54 Struck by Luck (A Riding   101
    Pass on Surprise in the
    Grass)

55 Up and Running   103
    (Limericked Lines on a Foal
    That Shines)

56 Winning Ways (Rhyming   104
    Frilly on My Arab Filly)

57 The Show-Off (A Horse of   106
    Dreams Is All He Seems)

58 Warning Signs and   109
    Traveling Whines (On
    Finding Grace Along the
    Way)

59 Sojourners (A Rhyme   112
    Supplied on a Peaceful Ride)

60 Unbroken   114

    About the Author   117

Horseplay Secrets

Learning

in

Rhyme

from

Equines Sublime

1

Come to Me

Leave the herd, and come to me,
And we will roam the wilds with glee.
Gallop from the greenest field,
And so become my strongest shield.

We have waited, right or wrong,
To discover joys lifelong.
The trail awaits us, end unknown,
With secret beauty yet unshown.

We'll mend the miles and race the breeze,
A-galloping beneath the trees.
So carry me beyond mundane,
As I hold tightly to your mane.

2

A Gentle Touch

(Basking Beats Tasking)

A bright blue sky bids us outdoors
'Mid warmer winds and equine snores.
We'd like to saddle up for flight
In fanciful fantastic light,
To celebrate the sunny spring
With landmarks softly listening.

But statues still are all we find,
With limbs and tails and manes
entwined.
No contract have we thus to ride –
To bring these peaceful ones inside.
By listening, we learn, of course,
To curl up gently with a horse.

3

My Daughter's First Love

(A Poetic Lead Line on Her Best Valentine)

I bought my girl a Valentine,
When she was only twelve.
This one was of divine design,
Not something off the shelf.

He was a little jumpy, sure.
That's how he stole her heart.
His racy manners, her allure –
I knew they'd never part.

He'd strut his stuff for her to see;
She'd sit upon the fence
And watch, as he'd cavort with glee,
In passion most intense.

He soon gave her the run-around
To demonstrate his pride.
This handsome one, without a sound,
He took her for a ride.

One day, he dumped her in a flash,
Humility's crash course.
I answered, though it sounded brash,
"Go get back on that horse!"

She earned his love and gained his trust
In each and every gait.
And though I know, grow up she must,
He's still her favorite date.

4

Far Afield

(A Limericked Ride 'Cross the Countryside)

Let's go for a ride in the green,
Where destiny beckons unseen.
We'll gallop the plain,
No rules to explain,
Vacation from daily routine.

The most sacred wonders, we share,
No scorn or remorse to beware.
Ourselves, all alone,
No deadlines, no phone –
We gallop the gulch with a prayer.

The rest of the herd worries not.
We smile at the wind at a trot.

The solace we hold,

Far greater than gold,

Resides in our own secret spot.

5

Land Mines

We live beside a danger zone,
So watch before you tread.
And when the grass is overgrown,
The obstacles embed.

Bare feet are not advisable,
As everybody knows,
And things unrecognizable
May seep between your toes.

We live out in the countryside,
Where animals are found.
So watch before you slip and slide,
And step over that mound!

6

Detangling with Delight

(Rhyming Lots on Losing Knots)

A feral foal will stand at rest –
Allowing grooming, no protest.
Though burrs be tangled in his mane,
His energies he may contain.

He'll hover there for human care,
With equine heart a-beating fair.
No stranger may approach him thus,
But those who bend to earn his trust.

Such high horizons beckon all,
Where courage may send fear a-fall.
These interactions school the soul,
Eliminating crowd's control.

We need to bridle burning pasts
To build a legacy that lasts.
For saddled with concerns untamed,
We merely march in meter, maimed.

The wisest man knows how to live.
To temper stress, one must forgive.
May sound a bit naïve, but true,
That crossing boundaries builds view.

7

Midwinter Mirth

(A Limericked Word on My Favorite Herd)

No misty magic tops the mirth.

In fact, no wonder on the earth

Eclipses joy in fields of frost,

As horses' hoofprints mark criss-cross

In sweetest snow, for all they're worth.

8

El Santo

(Saddled with Responsibility)

The guardian I trust the most,
Beatified from coast to coast,
May poke his nose in everything,
While babysitting in the ring.

He has been known to tell a tale,
To shoot the breeze
    and bring the mail.
If youngsters wander out of bounds,
He'll holler his unearthly sounds.

To dictate discipline, he'll call.
To balance battles, save a fall,

This tattletale is right on course,

Because he is a saintly horse.

9

Paging the Prime Veterinarian

(Three Questions in Rhyme on a Horse Past Her Prime)

Three things I have wondered
    and not understood –
A triad of questions I'd ask,
    if I could.

First off, I'd inquire for equines I love:
Has God built a stable for them up above?
I've heard that in Heaven
    the horses can fly.
What happens to animals after they die?

How long must a dearly loved mare

remain sore,

Reluctantly leaving

    the sheltered stall door?

What days, months or years

      will she hover afield,

Once alpha, now weaker,

    to others to yield?

And how will we know

    when her time is at hand?

How can we be sure

    we won't misunderstand?

Humanity questions,

    and hearts break apart,

Considering issues no doctor can chart.

She'll gallop again in the clouds,

    I am sure,

With flying lead changes

    and energy pure.

One day, I will join her

    to leap without end,

And frolic on high
    with my great golden friend.

Three things I have wondered
    and not understood –
A triad of questions I'd ask,
    if I would.

Thank God the Creator
    is faithful and good.
May He intervene,
    where I never could.

10

Dandy Day

It's a dandy day for a turnout,
A wonderful day in the field,
A perfect day to beat burnout,
As sweet dandelions are revealed.

I promise I'll give you a ride, dear,
If you will allow me to stay.
The grasses are growing beside here,
And they taste much sweeter than hay.

The dew of the morning has rested
On each lovely blade that I munch.
So don't feel that I have protested,
But please come and ride after lunch.

11

Gearing Up

(A Limericked Ride on a Colt with Pride)

Sweet transmission. Never fear,

As they switch from gear to gear.

Each transition's smooth and soft,

While he holds his tail aloft.

Wonder where they'll go from here.

First, they walk with measured pace,

Till they trot with simple grace.

Then the canter, whirling gait,

Galloping before too late.

One day, they may pirouette.

As they pass the judge's booth,

Rider and her handsome youth,

Qualifying scores they'll seek:

Halt at "X," salute, and peek,

Trying not to be uncouth.

Sweet admission, just the two –

Saddled up – look how they grew!

Dreaming of the gate and ring,

As they run and fly and fling.

Let's wait and enjoy the view.

12

Launched Again

(An Acrostic in Rhyme)

Loretta was lovely for sure,

Astride with her clean manicure,

Until underneath brewed a buck –

No warning, so quick, just her luck.

Catastrophe struck, as she flew,

Her helmet removed for her 'do.

Each onlooker stood, daring dread.

Does fashion count, heels over head?

At last, the equestrienne rose.

Good grief! There she stood,

    wiping nose.

Another day, she would return

In fashions pristine, cash to burn –

No true horse sense lessons to learn.

13

Bally-hue

With psychedelic patterned coat,
His tail a-flip and mane afloat –
A living statuary proud,
He gallops motionless 'mid crowd.

Elusive though his spirit be,
No shame may fade his gaiety.
Restarting rainbow's wondrous glow,
He prances proudly, off to show.

Aye, could it be he knows the cause
For which he prances without pause?
As now this technicolor steed
Displays his daunt for others' need.

So, riderless, yet on the edge,

Imagination pays its pledge.

One day, he'll grace another home,

This happy horse with colored chrome.

14

Have You Herd?

(A Rhyme Past-Due on a Wonderful Crew)

Have you heard about the herd?
It's my very favorite word.
Though you may think it absurd,
It's where I am most self-assured.

The herd admits without password.
There, pure acceptance is conferred.
Equine affection may be stirred,
And no one must be massacred.

In other crowds, where I've transferred,
It seems another is preferred.

Perhaps their vision may be blurred,

And they may realize afterward.

I tried to sing once, like a bird;

Instead of crooning, I just slurred.

So I departed, thus deterred,

To reconnect where best inferred.

And now I huddle with the herd –

By far, the best four-letter word.

15

Royalty Spoilty

(Limericked Joy for a True Blue Boy)

My boy looks beautiful in blue,

Though he's a royal pain. It's true.

He'll jump the moon

To any tune,

But every month, he'll toss a shoe.

My boy is handsomest in teal.

This color lights his orbs of steel.

In indigo,

He's apropos,

But turquoise does his light reveal.

In cobalt, cornflower or ice,

My boy is dashing, ultra-nice –

His shining mane,

Almost profane,

Is every filly's paradise.

Blue halters, sheets and saddle pad

Make him a stylishly dressed lad.

He fairly gleams

With color schemes

As gallant as Sir Galahad.

My boy looks beautiful in blue,

Though he's a royal pain. It's true.

He stole my scene

And all my green

To leave my statements all past-due.

16

Fragile Finery

(The Cost of Grace and Glory)

A lovely filly, fine, first class

Without question, bonny lass,

Pranced arenas, without par,

Ever graceful superstar –

Leaving others at impasse.

With perfect braids and flexing poll,

She lured the judges to extol

Lovely form and elegance –

Poise and beauty, all at once,

Capturing both heart and soul.

Despite her winning ways, alas,

This finest filly, Sassafras,

Token flaw she did possess:

Refinement carried to excess.

For she was made of fragile glass.

17

A Cloud Unveiled

His glory days had long blown by,
This creamy horse, straight from the sky,
When she discovered love again,
A-nuzzling his ivory mane.

Although Cloud's back was ever swayed,
He promptly stood to let her braid,
And marched her twice around the pond,
Devoted with a heart most fond.

A Quarter Horse, long past his game,
He quickly to her heart took aim.
She rescued this one and his pal,
A pure white gelding, known as Al.

These dirty white boys held their court
In highest fashions for their sport.
With polka dots and fancy trims,
They proudly pranced on ancient limbs.

Two pensioners, beyond belief,
They willingly turned o'er new leaf.
They sprouted wings, at least in heart,
But couldn't bear to be apart.

Now Cloud has gone alone ahead.
Arthritic longings he has shed.
Perhaps he prances in the sky
Through thunderheads aloft on high.

His comrade, Albert, Sir the Lame,
May linger, nickering his name,
And search the pasture, ne'er to find
His equine partner, Cloud the Blind.

Inseparable through they'd be
For years until eternity,

Now Albert strolls a solo stride

Without Cremello horse to guide.

For cloudy eyes of palest blue

Have since regained their light and hue.

This noble gentle equine friend

Will gallop pastures without end.

18

Great Green Grub

What is it that you crave to munch?

Perhaps a pretzel, peanuts, punch.

You may choose chocolate, chips, or cake.

What lures you to increased intake?

My favorite foods to munch all day

Are timothy, alfalfa, hay.

Of course, an apple is a treat –

A carrot, peppermint, not meat.

Although the herd may buck and wail,

I plan to stand here at the bale.

When spring's green grass may yet

appear,

Then I may step away from here.

19

No Wrest for the Wicked

The fox-hunting season began,
As horses and hounds swiftly ran –
The boy's name was Reed,
The pony's Stampede.
Grandfather held on with one hand.

Herein they began a quick trip,
As mini attempted to flip.
The little one wailed,
But honor prevailed,
As Senior lost not his strong grip.

20

Belly Up to the Bale

(A Rhyming Form Amid the Storm)

For breakfast in the field, we find
Dear friends with manes and tails
entwined.
The sun has faded like a coin,
And winter rushes to purloin.

Tradition calls, with instinct merged,
As fillies here have quite converged.
The biggest bale of hay in store –
"If only we might have some more."

Like buddies in the local pub,

They gather here to rub and scrub,

To sing their song, as storms prevail

And belly right up to the bale.

21

Private Dining

(A Filly's Rhyme on Suppertime)

The city lights, they touch her not,

For beauty thus need not be sought.

Alone, she savors stolen treats,

Ere others join, with pounding beats.

She makes an entrance out of doors,

Just filled with joy, she yet implores.

Perchance this time she need not share

Her bounty feast in open air.

22

Fairly Fall

(A Trip on the Trail)

Leaving home for just a while,

And heading for the trail in style –

With hands on reins,

Held close to manes,

We carve our joys in single file.

No scary stories taunt us here,

A-galloping with those held dear.

With softest cues,

We banish blues

In golden autumn's atmosphere.

23

A Great Sport

(Poetic Scan from a Loyal Fan)

My favorite athlete is tall
But wears no uniform at all.
My childhood dreams appear in him,
A wonder far beyond all whim.

His hair could rival Samson's mane,
Unscissored, difficult to tame.
He'll cast a glance to catch my eye,
Confused that others pass him by.

A champion in his own right,
I love to watch this one take flight.
It's almost scary – watch him race,

Inviting others to give chase.

And what comes after may surprise;
For reasons I cannot surmise,
He'll stop and stoop for me to climb
For quiet road trip, one more time.

His purpose, though he seem untamed,
A-frolicking so unashamed,
Is found fulfilled between us too,
Not just collecting ribbons blue.

24

Halter-Skelter

(Wisdom from the Wild)

Sun's soft ray and pasture play
Simply take our breath away.
Colts and fillies run and romp.
Soon the horseflies they will stomp.

Yanking halters, chewing manes,
Living free from ropes and reins,
Horses practice tug-of-war
In their paradise outdoor.

In their frolic free-for-all,
Equines rear up, strong and tall.
Here, untethered, youngsters grow,

Chestnut coats in sun aglow.

Someday soon, their lives will change,
And their schedules rearrange –
Trained by gesture, cue, and word,
As they long for treasured herd.

25

My Guy

(A Simple List to Give the Gist)

My favorite male is filled with charm.
I might tattoo him on my arm.
Why do I love him most, of course?
He bests all men, my little horse.

When e'er he sees me, he high-tails
To greet me and hear my regales.
Although he may not understand,
He as a listener is grand.

No foul language does he speak,
Nor does his temper seem to pique.
Fidelity's his strongest suit.

(He's gelded, so the point is moot.)

Unlike most men a gal might know,
He cuddles with no quid pro quo.
This handsome one is strong and sure.
His macho ego is secure.

He smiles with ease for our close-ups
And never ever interrupts.
And with a little exercise,
This blessed beast may win a prize.

Of all the guys in all the earth,
One little horse renews his worth.
This bold, bright equine is my dear,
As long as I shall have him here.

26

Jumpin' Jehosaphat

(Limericked Sweeps on a Horse That Leaps)

Jehosaphat can jump. That's true.

This gelding pilots us straight through.

We go off-road,

Aim for payload,

And Big J leaps into the blue.

Though Mom has never learned to jump,

Jehosaphat takes any bump.

They reach the rails;

He simply sails

And pilots Mom without a thump.

27

Private Moments

(Recalling the Birth of a Foal)

What scene can match the wondrous
worth
Of witnessing an equine birth?

Eleven months of biding time,
Beloved mare, just past her prime:
We watch her bloom and gently wait,
While grazing by the pasture gate.

Her form grows rounder by the day.
Will it be chestnut, bay or gray?
Her spirit quiets, as she grows;
We wonder if perhaps she knows.

As her maternity draws near,
We cannot help but interfere.
Into the night, we stand and spy.
How does she sense that we're nearby?

Eventually, the barn grows still,
And in the air, we feel a thrill.
A quiet scene then stirs my soul:
Our mare displays her newborn foal.

She nudges him to help him stand,
In this, their private holy land.
We hold our breath, as they proceed,
And mother helps her infant feed.

It baffles us to see the scene,
This pure escape from things obscene.
As nature educates the mare,
Instinctively, she learns to care.

The dam and foal become acquainted.

We observe the scene untainted.
Tumbling then, he comes to rest,
As mother keeps her watch, unstressed.

Someday he'll train for exercise,
But for tonight, we realize
This moment captures all we know,
As Heaven visits us below.

What scene can match the wondrous
worth
Of witnessing an equine birth?
Creation whispers; we can hear
The Maker ever drawing near.

28

Reunion Aloft

(Farewell to a Friend)

The day has come,
The clouds foretold –
Another chum will join the fold.

Our hearts may fall
To watch him go.
We miss his call,
The bleached beau.

A partner dear
Calls him aloft.
We cannot hear
The whisper soft.

We witness not
Reunion's glow,
As comrades trot,
Their joy to show.

His limbs are strong.
Behold, his gait.
He strides to song
With running mate.

Their chalky coats,
White and champagne,
Do fairly float
In flight, free rein.

Without a word,
But winged, fair,
They join the herd
In open air.

29

Jump-Starts on Smarts

(Pastoral Wisdom from the Pasture)

In conversations with a friend,

We swap ideas and comprehend

The truths of life,

An end to strife –

And our opinions recommend.

We often think outside the box;

Press close to God – see, here He walks.

For smart are we,

Here in our glee,

With oil of wonder, our life rocks.

30

A Stroll That's Droll

This morning, as we were out walking,

My pony and I were a-talking.

He let out a neigh,

But I said, "No way!"

And our friends thought us all laughing-

stocking.

31

Stocking Up

(A Rhyming Ridge Too Close to the Bridge)

The horn may sound,
    And hounds may bay.
Companions hunt for words to say.
We watch for hours at her side,
Awaiting yet the coming tide.

The fever strikes.
    The lymph nodes swell.
Perhaps the clock may only tell.
I cling fast to a fraying rope,
And in the melting mud, hold hope.

It breaks my heart to see her fall –
Another close call, after all.

32

Minis and Whinnies

(Limericked Courses on Tiny Horses)

The miniature horses are cute.

They pull carts and wagons to boot.

For folks great and small,

The minis enthrall

With darlingness most absolute.

A horse may be tiny or tall,

While ponies aren't horses at all.

Though some are confused

Or merely bemused,

Small horses fit two to a stall.

And here is what puzzles us so,

Attending each horse driving show:

The minis are strong,

A-wheeling along,

When judges say, "Ready, set, go."

33

Just Arrived

(A Foal Extols an Outdoor Stroll)

Hey, Mama, let's go out to play,

Although I have not learned to neigh.

I'm weak in the knees,

But I'll trail you with ease,

'Cause it's my discovery day.

I'll follow you out in the grass

And try not to merely harass,

While you, my food source,

Romp and play as a horse,

Until we both fall, out of gas.

34

A Daily Dip

What summer sport may more joy bear
Than puddle plodding, mud to wear?
Two four-star friends may munch and
muse
And splish and splash and standing
snooze.

Their lifelines have been etched in white,
Two decades plus without a fight.
What other pair may boast the same –
No bickering or passing blame?

Though fetlock scratches may appear,
They fret it not, companions dear.
As younger equines run and romp,

They swish their tails and simply stomp.

The virile herd may spook and shy,
But these pale gents don't bat an eye.
For they have witnessed so much more.
Perhaps they've seen it all before.

35

First Flight

Three years ago, he hit the ground.
I marveled at the wonder found.
This boy bewitched me from the start.
One shake of mane: he held my heart.

Resolved to ride, I watched him grow,
While waiting, cherishing his glow.
I'd write of riding him one day,
And worry-free, we'd run away.

Thus, desperate for a saddled trip,
I cultivated horsemanship.
Year after year dragged slowly by
Until the day when we would fly.

At last, I climbed upon his back

And cued him softly on the track.

We jogged one way, then back again,

A traveled pair at last. Amen!

36

Green Lessons

(A Poetic Reflection on Riding Correction)

I used to think I knew a lot.
My horses nearly were self-taught.
We'd pirouette, right on the spot,
Until this sorrel colt I bought.

I used to think myself quite smart,
My equitation, work of art,
Until this colt, he stole my heart
And upended my apple cart!

I never stood a single chance.
He looked at me, a simple glance,

And my resolve turned happenstance,
As I embarked on new finance.

I used to think that I could ride.
My ribbons, I displayed with pride
From horse show classes, far and wide,
Until he carried me, wide-eyed.

I used to think I had some skill,
Until this youngster of goodwill
Began to gallop from standstill.
I hollered like a whippoorwill!

So now I've come to know my place,
Although this is a change of pace,
Discovering a saving grace.
My colt and I could win a race!

Although we're smitten, this is true.
I'm learning not to overdo.
My hands and feet will softly cue,
Preventing further whoop-de-doo.

37

Running with the Right Herd

My friends, they're not so cool at all.
I think they need an overhaul,
An extrication from the mall
And tutoring in protocol.

Their manicures are without flaw;
It ought to be against the law –
Their afternoons spent at the spa,
Where every day is Mardi Gras.

They need some soil beneath their nails,
From strolling scenic nature trails
And scavenging at rummage sales
For bridles, halters, feeding pails.

My friends' ideals set me asunder,
Baffle me and make me wonder:
As they browse for pretty plunder,
Do I dare to steal their thunder?

For I am rich beyond their dreams.
My muddy face, it fairly gleams.
My life's much more than e'er it seems,
For I have won the herd's esteem.

This graceful gentry does not care
What labels or designs I wear,
Or if my jeans should sport a tear.
Their noses arch not in the air.

We plunge and romp in mud and dust,
For that is how we learn to trust,
And even if our hair is mussed,
Our dear companionship is just.

My proper friends are not so swell,
And this is how we all can tell.

If I approach with equine smell,
They curtly bid me fond farewell.

38

Still Standing

She's standing still,
Against her will,
Although she'd rather
Run for thrill.

Our mare of gold
Is growing old,
And yet her story
Must be told.

Her motor stirs;
No need for spurs.
She longs to run,
As she prefers.

And yet, she slows
Before my whoas.
Her energy now
Ebbs and flows.

I pray she'll stay
Another day,
For I delight
To hear her neigh.

39

Sight-Mare

(Seeing Through Blindness)

I'm sure I have been here before,
Though I perceive it not.
Equine apologies and more
May not obscure the spot.

While waiting for a pathway stroll,
The world one day grew dark.
Now worry crowds my searching soul,
E'er seeking hopeful spark.

To question why my sight has fled
Won't hasten my parole.
Instead, I listen well while led

And wait for healthy foal.

With rock-resolve, I make my way,
Accompanied in trust.
My dear companion leads each day.
To follow her I must.

I carry forth no knot of hate.
Let this become my lot.
Although rheumatic, more of late,
I find a grassy spot.

Sclerotic scarring dims my view.
For this, I've often cried.
My owners forgo rendezvous,
For they no longer ride.

So this is how I met my match,
The finest friend of all.
For when they open pasture latch,
I listen for her call.

My sight-mare pal is destined here.

Without her, I'd be lost.

Her presence energizes dear,

Though she knows not the cost.

40

Untacked in Fact

My sweet young friend is in the swim.
I cannot get enough of him.
He bids me to his back to swing,
I swell with pride and with him sing.

So effortlessly, holding mane,
I find no need for bit or rein.
No thrashing, dashing, spook or shy –
Our company does satisfy.

A little knowledge may have worth,
But in the herd, more down to earth,
Abuse of power may draw ire.
A colt may bite; a hoof may fire.

Vindictive values know no place.

Our tempers vanish, as we race.

We gather, horse and humankind,

And there our souls are intertwined.

Discoveries of daily truth,

Displayed by finest friends in youth,

May lead to habits of high praise

For Him who grants delightful days.

41

From the Dust

Her pony had a hissy fit.
She never saw it coming.
He reared and bucked, and that was it.
Then he was off and running.

Mid-show, she rose and coughed up dust.
Thank God, she was unhurt.
She knew, to mount again she must,
Not wallow in the dirt.

She held her breath and climbed aboard
Her impudent blood-bay.
They cleared the hurdles, soared and scored,
The champions of the day.

42

A Running Start

(Lyrics Penned for a Truest Friend)

My favorite friend is tall and strong;
He takes me where I don't belong.
We share our secrets and our joys –
With him, I need no other boys.

You caught my heart.
You caught my hand.
With a running start,
On you I'll land.

My favorite friend has earned my trust.
We leave all others in the dust.
He doesn't scratch or pick his nose.

He never worries 'bout his clothes.

You caught my heart.
You caught my hand.
With a running start,
On you I'll land.

My favorite friend has golden hair,
And I have never heard him swear.
He winks at me, and life is good.
I've never been misunderstood.

You caught my heart.
You caught my hand.
With a running start,
On you I'll land.

I know he'll never cheat on me,
Because our partnership is free.
By now, you've figured out, of course:
My dearest friend, he is my horse.

You caught my heart.
You caught my hand.
With a running start,
On you I'll land.

43

Low-Maintenance

(A Poetic Presuming on Personal Grooming)

I spend my summers in the dirt;
The pasture is my spot.
With sweat and grass stains on my shirt,
I gallop my hotshot.

In tank and jeans, both day and night,
And slimy horse-lick facial,
My torso tan, the rest stark white,
I'm vertically biracial!

I never sport a pedicure.
In fact, quite the reverse.

I keep my feet contained, secure,
In paddock boots and spurs.

However, I have one left toe
That's twice its normal size,
Because a Thoroughbred I know
Stomped me instead of flies.

My manicure is reverse-French,
With soil, instead of polish.
It carries still a tell-tale stench
To put off or demolish.

I rarely paint or file my nails.
I simply let them grow.
Persnickety is for upscales,
While I am on the go.

I toss my locks into a band
And simply let them fly,
With many an unruly strand
That falls into one eye –

Or tuck my hair into a cap
To keep it up, of course.
Long hair can be a handicap
When working with a horse.

My clothes, they're not the latest mode
Of fashion or of style,
But they protect me from the road
When cantering a mile.

My leather boots have traveled long;
They bear a layer of crust,
But that is where I best belong,
In deep terrain or dust.

Low-maintenance could be the word
For my own regimen.
And yet, I spit-shine my whole herd.
Just take a look at them.

Each mane or tail shines in the sun,

In vanity displayed.

They stand, show-ready, every one.

My horses have it made!

44

Playing It Cool

The fairest fillies on the farm

May with the frost take no alarm.

They find it fine ,

Design divine –

To laugh at winter's chilly charm.

45

Ready to Go

You want to know what's on my mind?
The show-truck left. I'm left behind.
I'm disagreeable and sour,
And growing more so by the hour.

I find it difficult to smile.
My pals grow absent by the mile.
A catnap may be what I need –
Perhaps a handful of sweet feed.

I'd like to take the plunge and show,
To demonstrate the skills I know.
An underdog? No way! Not me!
I'll pirouette at liberty.

In fact, the opposite is true.
I'd surely take the ribbon blue.
Please let me play. I'll do my best
To stun the judges in my test.

Don't make me stay here and pretend
Essential training, flex and bend.
I'll canter, swap leads and halt square,
If you will only take me there.

46

The Master's Marvel

Yesterday, Sir Spring had sprung.
The earth was vital, verdant, young.
He didn't see it flip its flow
To fill the field with falling snow.

A fancy foal, he yet extolled,
Ere aging days should make him old –
"Hey, here I am," he softly spoke.
"Why has Sir Spring gone up in smoke?"

Perhaps tomorrow we'll make hay.
Today we'll frolic, roll, and play.
As jumbled seasons mingle here,
May we not miss a moment's cheer.

47

My Lifeguard

She doesn't wear a nose of white.
Her skin is never tanned.
And yet, she runs to save my life,
Out there in no-man's land.

I saunter into danger
And am suddenly surrounded,
When friend or foe or stranger
Leaves me confused and confounded.

I call out for my lifeguard,
And she hurries to my aid.
Be it super-stud or blowhard,
My lifeguard's unafraid.

When others seek to do me harm,

She races to my side.

My alpha mare, queen of the farm,

Then takes me for a ride.

48

Mystified

A foal is born, and so he grows,
Until we head for rings and shows.
The trail awaits, and so do we,
My handsome chestnut colt and me.

Today, we saddled him for once,
Without a glitch, no bucks or stunts.
In tack he's never worn before,
He modeled like a matador.

This horse, he has me mystified.
I cannot hardly wait to ride.
We're smitten to the core, we two,
Awaiting saddle-borne debut.

49

Rescued by the Ride

A never-ending sense of trust
Is strengthened by the whirling dust.
And when dear friends together roam,
We're cheered before the long walk
home.

We tread the trail, as it unfolds,
And autumn turns the greens to golds.
The lead horse surely sets the pace.
The journey will our ills erase.

Arriving at the barn again,
We raise a toast to where we've been.
Then, tempted by a banquet sweet,
We mark a perfect day complete.

50

My Dirty Secret

No doubt, the magnificent
    moments of all
And summertime memories,
    both great and small,
Are oft found in solace,
    as nature observes,
For these are occasions
    that quiet our nerves.

When rumors may shake us
    and make us to fret,
Spontaneous uprisings
    cause a cold sweat –
'Tis then we escape
    to the dust and the grime,

For days in the pasture
     are ne'er wasted time.

So take me away
     from the ring and the race.
And let me escape
     to my own private place,
Where sharing the meadow
     with those I adore
Rejuvenates me
     for what life has in store.

51

Bee-ware

(A Limericked Scheme on a Near-Broken Dream)

We came to the end of a ride,

Each gait marked with optimum stride,

Then went to unwind

On a roadway tree-lined,

Still coaxing our ponies astride.

We walked for a few lazy laps,

While keeping our mounts under wraps.

Just then,

   in a flash,

My pony did dash

And knocked me into a time lapse.

It seems that a hornet attack

Transformed my sweet mount

    to a hack.

He bucked,

    and he kicked,

And I could not predict

How hard on the ground I would smack.

Twelve broken bones later,

    I crawled.

My body was then overhauled.

For more than a year,

I stood by, unclear,

With riding no more so enthralled.

Once more, I remounted that colt,

Aware he might suddenly bolt.

No bees in our range,

But time for a change,

I almost gave up from the jolt.

At last, I was ready to learn.

My sweet mare than gave me a turn.

She walked in slow queue

Until we both knew

The respect we two longed then to earn.

52

Stardust and Snowflakes

(A Winter's Day for Bay and Gray)

On Gypsy wings, the wind, she sings,
Her timely tune to share.
Each feathered fetlock softly clings
Against the frosted air.

The icy breeze, she dances free,
As equines watch and wait.
A mystic wave may meet them there
Beside the frozen gate.

And I believe the wild ones weave
An ever-present truth.
For here they dare not to deceive

The blinding bloom of youth.

A swath of stardust meets each mane,
Despite the daylight's glare,
And each receives, yet can't contain
The joy beyond compare.

53

Capping It Off

The horseman is headless, they say.

He rides on a spirited bay –

His hair in the breeze,

    as he gallops with ease.

He's stored his crash helmet away.

The horseman, he must use his head,

And not by appearance be led.

Just strap on his cap

For victory lap,

So vultures above won't be fed.

54

Struck by Luck

(A Riding Pass on Surprise in the Grass)

We galloped 'cross the countryside,
The perfect afternoon trail ride.
Beside a creek, we paused to rest
And lounged awhile in grassy nest.

Our horsey posse was content.
To sit a spell was our intent.
We sighed to see a day so fair,
Empowered by fresh country air.

The horses drank and gaily grazed,
As on the shore, we simply lazed.

We picked up clovers, just for fun,
And plucked the leaves off, one by one.

"He loves me, yes; he loves me not,"
Provided our best food for thought,
Until I found a four-leaf clover,
There beside our ride layover.

Suddenly, like chimpanzees,
We were all on hands and knees,
Hunting through the wild field
To find another lucky yield.

To our surprise, the land was filled
With four-leaf clovers, yet untilled.
What caused this region to enchant,
Just downstream from the power plant?

55

Up and Running

(Limericked Lines on a Foal That Shines)

Excuse us, if we stop and stare,

But your first steps show savoir-faire.

With style and speed,

You're guaranteed

To grab attention everywhere.

Although the world is new to you,

Instinctively, you capture view.

And none too late,

We celebrate

To see life's miracle come true.

56

Winning Ways

(Rhyming Frilly on My Arab Filly)

My little Arab horse trots by,
Her graceful neck arched to the sky,
That happy flag tail raised up high,
To entertain all passers-by.

This desert beauty, chestnut gold,
A poetry live to behold,
May now be only two years old,
But soon her training will unfold.

One day, she'll learn to sport her tack,
To carry me upon her back.
And then, my lovely maniac
Will prance for judges, run the track.

Although she may be hard to catch,

A-galloping the pasture patch,

Her stamina no colt can match.

Opponents she will soon dispatch.

She'll jump the hurdles, swap her lead,

And live up to her winning breed.

The crowd stampede, she will exceed

And earn the ribbons, guaranteed.

57

The Show-Off

(A Horse of Dreams Is All He Seems)

The year's first show began our quest

To put our gelding to the test.

This apparition on patrol

Took every turn to rock and roll.

Apologizing we are not

For putting others on the spot.

They came to play, and so did we,

My daughter and her horse and me.

This Thoroughbred of darkest bay

Adores the limelight on display.

A competition draws him out
Eliminating judges' doubt.

His secret lies within his chest
With heart that beats above the rest.
A well-placed fence is opportune,
And for his girl,
    he'll jump the moon.

The season opener, of course,
He took in stride, this glory horse.
Though twilight beckoned, no retreat,
He leapt to win, the course complete.

He lost the right lead, but returned
And ripped the runaway unspurned.
His pilot, decked in tailored threads,
Flashed pearly teeth and turned all
heads.

As sunset crept across the clouds,
And battle scars befell the crowds,

We packed our tack to homeward crawl

And hang his ribbons on his stall.

58

Warning Signs and Traveling Whines

(On Finding Grace Along the Way)

The show invitation said "Nine."

Departing at eight, we'd be fine.

Then, spotting the cones

And road closure zones,

We murmured to miss the deadline.

A repaving crew put us out,

While signaling us to reroute.

Though drowsy, we drove

Past foliage-filled grove.

The trailer behind bounced about.

A slight indiscretion, wrong turn –

We rumbled along at slow burn,

With nothing to do

But plod along through

And recheck the clock –

     live and learn.

So swindled were we and our freight.

The show fees we'd lose.

     None would wait.

And right from the gun,

We'd miss all the fun,

For we could not accelerate.

Still, somehow, our joy we re-found,

With autumn arriving all 'round.

We gave up the war,

Not irked anymore,

And noticed Creation's background.

An old covered plankway stretched west,

Thus bridging the gap o'er a crest.
We drove 'cross the bog,
As sun lifted fog,
Observing the scenery with zest.

We pointed the rig from frontier,
Surprising a full herd of deer.
Like water, they poured.
They bounded and soared –
A vanishing sight souvenir.

And although we scratched from the
show,
We made our way home in a glow,
Unloading our mounts
And pleased to announce
More fun than the whole rodeo.

59

Sojourners

(A Rhyme Supplied on a Peaceful Ride)

I rode along beribboned curls,
Abandoned by titanic girls.
A broken stripe, it marked the pace,
As we tore up the empty space.

My maned companion, Zanzibar,
He carried me to lands afar.
His hoofbeats rattled in accord
On silent pathways, thus ignored.

The highway kept to us alone,
A sweet long-distance chaperone,

As there we journeyed, shore to shore,
To leave our home forevermore.

60

Unbroken

They run as one and jump the gun
From crack of dawn to setting sun.
A branch will crack. Sound the attack!
And off they fly in fondest fun.

A closer crowd I never saw,
This wild bunch, quick on the draw.
They turn en masse and carry on,
And gallop off, till they're long gone.

Then, spent, they fall upon the dust,
Abandoning their wanderlust,
Each resting on another's mane
Until they rise to race again.

They run as one and jump the gun
From crack of dawn to setting sun.
A branch will crack. Sound the attack!
And off they fly in fondest fun.

Few kindred spirits, they'll permit
Their company to benefit.
We scale the fence and take a stroll
To witness strength under control.

Another year, and they will train
To wear a saddle, bridle, rein.
Their spirits strong will long remain
To earn the honors they'll attain.

They run as one and jump the gun
From crack of dawn to setting sun.
A branch will crack. Sound the attack!
And off they fly in fondest fun.

About the Author

Linda Ann Nickerson is an avid equestrian, breeding and raising sport horses and competing in both English and Western riding.

An award-winning poet and prolific writer, holding a B.A. in English and an M.S. in Journalism, Linda Ann Nickerson has worked as a professional writer for more than three decades. She has also taught creative writing classes.

Linda Ann Nickerson writes news and feature columns for several well-known websites. Her published portfolio includes well over 5,000 web articles, as well as countless print pieces.

Blogs owned by Linda Ann Nickerson include:

- Delightfully Amiss: Berzerkians Gone Amok and Finding the Funk in Dysfunction

- Heart of a Ready Writer

- Nickers and Ink

- Practically at Home

- The Mane Point: A Haven for Horse Lovers

- Working in Words

- and more.

Other titles by this author

- *25 Top Tips for Promoting Your Equestrian Event: Get the Herd Out*

- *Absent Nightmare Zinnias: Rhymed Acrostics from A to Z*

- *Stealing Wonder: A Rhyming Race to Capture Grace*

- *What's in Santa's Sleigh This Christmas?*

Readers are invited to follow Linda Ann Nickerson on Twitter (LindaAnnNickers) or Google+ (Linda Ann Nickerson) or to join the Nickers and Ink Facebook page.